The Spiritual Apprenticeship of a Curious Catholic

Jerry Hurtubise

ACTA
ASSISTING CHRISTIANS TO ACT
PUBLICATIONS

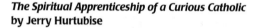

The Spiritual Apprenticeship of a Curious Catholic
by Jerry Hurtubise

Edited by Gregory F. Augustine Pierce
Cover design by Tom A. Wright
Cover art "Communion Cup" by Paula Wiggins, www.thespiritsource.com
Typesetting by Desktop Edit Shop, Inc.

Published by   ACTA Publications
              Assisting Christians To Act
              4848 N. Clark Street
              Chicago, IL 60640
              800-397-2282
              www.actapublications.com

The names of some of the people in this book have been changed to prevent any possible embarrassment on their part.

Library of Congress Catalog number: 2004117004
ISBN: 0-87946-283-3
Printed in the United States of America
Year 10 09 08 07 06 05
Printing 10 9 8 7 6 5 4 3 2 1

Contents

To Catherine,
through whose love
I have learned
to see.

A Note from the Publisher

Religious professionals (priests, nuns, brothers, monks, laypeople who work for the church) write most spiritual memoirs. That is just a fact. Most Catholics are not religious professionals. That is just another fact.

Most Catholics are lay people who live out their faith on their jobs, with their families, and in their communities and are seldom if ever asked to write about those experiences—especially from a religious or spiritual point of view.

The American Catholic Experience is a series of books that attempts to fill that void. These are short, accessible, provocative reflections by individual Catholics on their personal experience of God and Christianity and church and life. Each book in the series is organized around a different theme, but the author is free to organize his or her thoughts in whatever way seems to work.

The Spiritual Apprenticeship of a Curious Catholic is the first book in this series—and in many ways inspired it. When Jerry Hurtubise, a successful San Francisco attorney and lifelong Catholic first approached me about publishing his book, I saw immediately that it was well-written and deserved to be published. But who, I thought, would buy a book of spiritual memoirs by a layman—especially one who is not well-known outside his own community and profession? Then I thought, which comes first: Do we not publish spiritual material by laypeople because it doesn't sell, or does it not sell because we don't publish it?

I started thinking about other similar manuscripts that I turn down regularly because they don't exactly "fit" into our normal religious publishing categories, and I realized what they all had in common was that they were personal reflections about the various aspects of the experience of being Catholic in the United States in the last part of the twentieth and the first part of the twenty-first centuries. Why not publish a series of such books and see if we can discover an audience for them? Hence *The American Catholic Experience* series.

You will find Jerry Hurtubise's book to be a joy. He originally began it as a way of writing down the stories of his childhood and youth for his son Peter. This was especially important for Jerry because his own father had died when he was very young and never had the opportunity to share his stories with him. But the book quickly grew into an exploration of the people and events that had formed Jerry into the man that he is today, and he quickly realized that much of what had happened to him had been his "spiritual apprenticeship" as a Catholic.

I invite you to enjoy *The Spiritual Apprenticeship of a Curious Catholic* and seek out the other titles in The American Catholic Experience series. I believe you will receive "grace upon grace" (John 1:16) when you do.

Gregory F. Augustine Pierce
President and Co-Publisher
ACTA Publications
Chicago, Illinois

Introduction

No thirteen-year-old boy is prepared to accept the responsibilities of adulthood—especially in the dead of night. Nonetheless, this would be my destiny.

As my mother frantically tried to awaken me that night, I resisted, somehow knowing the dream in which I was burrowed would be my last as a child. Her hysteria was no match for my struggle to cling to my innocence.

The memory of the look on her face as she made her futile effort to restart my father's heart, however, is one that I can never erase. It is the moment when I was torn from childhood, and it has ever since prevented me from seeing the world with the perspective of a child.

When a child experiences the death of a parent, it is like being in a dark room and suddenly having a bright light turned on. After a certain period of resistance, the light prevails, even though it continues to hurt your eyes.

My grief at my dad's death was normal. Even though my memory of him grows fainter, he is still very much alive in me. My biggest single regret is that with his death passed untold the stories of his younger days and his own spiritual apprenticeship. How I wish he had written them down for me.

So from the beginning—at least as far back as I can convince my middle-age memory to travel—please allow me to share with you some of the lessons I learned and the characters I met in my own youth. These events blessed me with lingering seeds of kindness, planted by those willing to help a curious Catholic youngster discover and define himself.

Jerry Hurtubise
Winslow and Hurtubise
Attorneys-at-Law
San Francisco, California

Singing Elvis for Grandpa

My early memories are fragmented; bouncing freely like little balls of mercury:

...My brother Bob at bedtime, with his arsenal of fables, coaxing my heavy eyelids to finally fall.

...Ivy covered walls of a cloistered high school seminary separating my brother Paul from me.

...My sister Mary Ann stripping a bully of dignity after learning my stomach had been punched.

...Dad hoisting my brother Mark atop the dining room table to sing "He's Got the Whole World in His Hands" for clergy and (considerably) less distinguished guests.

...Me being propped up on that same stage and singing: "Mary had a little lamb. That's what she gets for sleeping in the barn!"

These oldest remembrances include images of a visit to a farm in Iowa, where I traveled with Mom when I was four or five years old. Dad must have stayed in Indiana to work. I cannot remember whether or not any of my siblings were with us.

When Elvis was performing "You Ain't Nothing but a Hound Dog" on the Ed Sullivan show, I was also singing it for passengers on a train bound for Cedar Rapids. We chugged alongside an immense string of water that my mother introduced to me as "Mrs. Ippi." The locomotive and river seemed to move in concert.

Upon our arrival, Uncle Lawrence lifted my tiny frame from the train, setting me down on Iowa soil for the first time and gently squeez-ing my soft city hands with his big farmer hands full of calluses. Amidst the excitement, I scanned my surroundings hoping to discover Grandpa Ward somewhere in the background. I had seen only two pictures of him, one taken at his wedding and the other at my mother's wedding. Up until that trip, my grandfather had always been spoken of in the present tense in our house. So if I got the impression that he was not at the train station to greet us because he chose to stay back readying his tackle box and fishing poles for the next morning, you can understand. In fact, Grandpa Ward had died a decade before I was born.

Waking up for the first time on an Irish farm in Iowa opened up an entirely new structure of reality for me.

Uncle Lawrence and Aunt Rita Mae's house was teaming with chil-dren. All twelve were dressed in their Sunday best to meet strangers who were somehow related to them. I met Grandma Ward for the first time. I remember being a little scared of her, but I relaxed when her smile transformed her wrinkled face.

≈

Waking up for the first time on an Irish farm in Iowa opened up an entirely new structure of reality for me. Outside was a theater of chil-dren playing, dogs scaring chickens, and cows and corn standing their ground.

I remember Kenny, my oldest cousin, the most. He was the rural equivalent of my bodyguard. This became evident early on when I ran outside for the first time and he scooped me up onto his broad shoulders before an attacking rooster could peck my little leg.

"The thing about farm animals, Half Pint," he warned as he set me back down on the ground, "is that you shouldn't move too quickly. Farm animals got to get familiar with you before they can trust you. They're kind of like people that way. Even that old cock will attack you if it feels threatened."

"I know Kenny, but I feel stupid being chicken of a chicken," I confessed.

"You're not chicken. You're a little boy who nearly got his leg pecked by a sharp rooster beak."

"I know, but what if that rooster attacks me again?"

"What if that cow over there decides not to come home after he jumps over the moon tonight?" he teased. "We won't have any milk tomorrow, now will we?"

He knelt down next to me after I flashed him a look of concern.

"Look, Half Pint, if you want to be a farmer, you must learn we don't worry much about questions beginning with *what if.* We got plenty on our plate dealing with *what is.*"

〜

Aunt Rita Mae would come ceremoniously into my room each night with a broom to play a nightly game of "sweep the bats." Even at that very young age, I somehow knew it would be a breach of etiquette not to participate in this rural equivalent of "monsters under the bed." It all appeared quite harmless to me until one night Aunt Rita Mae departed from game protocol and advised me to slowly move away from the bed and into the hallway.

I humored her by tiptoeing out of the room and watched from the hallway through a crack in the slightly open door. From there I saw her lift an entire bed with one hand and beat to death two large black bats with the other. One went quickly; the other struggled to stay alive. One final high-pitched squeal was my cue that it was safe to go back into the room.

After being put to bed, I clung to my pillow, counting the peaceful inhalations and exhalations of the cousin who had won permission to sleep with me that night and who obviously had not been affected in the least by the strange ordeal.

I continued to lay awake as a rainstorm bullied its way into and out of Allamakee County. As a gentle rain replaced the sound of the retreating thunder, I imagined Grandpa kneeling near the place where water first sprang forth on the earth. "Pay no mind how deep you dig, Jerry. The deeper the well, the sweeter the water!" he whispered.

A Kinder Garden

Indiana mothers have perfected the art of early morning offspring launching.

Indeed, at the crack of dawn, no Indianapolis 500 pit crew had anything over our own mom as she rotated bowls of oatmeal and scrambled eggs with one hand, while laying out school clothes with the other.

Before being enrolled in kindergarten, I studied the various nuances of this familial dance from a safe place in the corner of the kitchen, realizing that I would soon be the last in her arsenal of spinning plates.

As the last of my siblings was coaxed into the chill of an Indiana morning, my mother welcomed the deafening quiet as she plopped down on her favorite chair. After a few deep breaths, though, her radiant smile would always turn to me.

∽∽

Mom would have been the perfect poster parent for the "nurture" icon in the nature-nurture debate. To her, cultivating crops and children had much in common: The landscape would be barren of both without patient attention to detail.

She and I spent an appreciable amount of time together in her garden, and many seeds were planted—both above and below the surface.

For those planted below, water was judiciously measured each day. For me, words of wisdom were sparingly and specifically applied.

Then one autumn, I was snatched from my mother's garden and inducted into what she promised would be a "kinder garden."

≈

All my school clothes had adorned my three older brothers, respectively, but my shoes always had new soles because, as Dad put it, I was "stepping into the new world of higher education."

My senses were offended by the utilitarian architecture of the schoolhouse, as well as the pungent odor of floor wax. Instinctively, tears welled into my eyes, which were being assaulted by a landscape muddled in threatening symmetry—every hallway, every door, every adult, every kid looked exactly the same.

I discovered that Mom's promise of taking me to a "kinder garden" had been nothing more than a ruse. My apprehensive demeanor did not go undetected. Three children, voluntarily segregated in a corner of the classroom, stepped forward and convinced me to free my hand from my mother's hem and come play with them in the back of the room.

This single event would destroy any chance my psyche might ever have had of being hard-wired with racial prejudice, for all three kids were black. Of all the children, they understood the need to console me: one by holding my hand; another by offering a much-coveted green rubber frog; and one by promising instant best friend status in exchange for a simple promise to stop my incessant whimpering.

Their teaching about friendship, along with my mother's promise to return at the end of each day, made the experience of that new garden at least slightly less intimidating.

Forgive Me, Father, for I Have Really Sinned

S ister Francesca's attention was on preparing thirty-six of us sin-stained Catholic second graders to make our first confession. So committed was she to have her students ready to receive the pastor's absolution that she rigged a makeshift confessional by her desk where we could rehearse our contrition.

"Remember, children," she repeated yet again, "It is 'Bless me, Father, for I have sinned. This is my very first confession and these are my sins....'"

Anticipating our inevitable stage fright, Sister Francesca encouraged us to chronicle our transgressions on a piece of paper and if absolutely necessary to simply read our sins to the priest the next day. I suppose this was a confessional cheat sheet of sorts.

Sister advised us to examine our consciences. There we would discover that most of our sins came from violating one of God's Ten Commandments. Having no recollection of having lied, stole or killed anyone, much less coveting anything or taking the Lord's name in vain (whatever that meant), I found my shortcomings were most clearly tied to multiple violations of the Fourth Commandment: "Honor your father and your mother." Clearly falling short of the reasonable expectations of my parents, I had fudged countless times on prayer saying, bed making, table setting, dish drying, clothes folding, weed pulling, flower watering, trash emptying and dog-poop scooping.

～

Needing a break from such self-critical thinking (and countless dress rehearsals staged in a dark corner in our basement with my older siblings), I wandered down the street to play with my friend Randy Grell. Not of the Catholic persuasion, Randy was somewhat confused when I voiced some concern about whether or not my sins were so weak and insignificant that they were not even worth mentioning. His first inclination was to suggest I simply make up a few sins. This had the added benefit that I could then truthfully report lying to top off my list of transgressions.

His first inclination was to suggest I simply make up a few sins.

Randy's idea was intriguing, but lying to a priest simply for the purpose of having something to confess seemed to pose a more complicated moral dilemma than I was willing to entertain. Suddenly, Randy told me to follow him inside his house.

"Come quickly, before my father gets home," he commanded.

"Why?" I asked.

"I got an idea."

We made our way into his father's den. There stood an antique mahogany bookcase, and on the very top was a set of tightly bound classic books that looked as if they were sealed together.

"Catch me if I fall," Randy instructed as he balanced himself on a swivel chair.

From where I stood, I could see him open the front part of the set of classics, revealing a hollow inside. Sticking his hand toward the back, he pulled out what looked like a magazine. He threw it down to me, telling me to open it to the middle. With little effort, a *Playboy* centerfold, nearly half my size, unfolded in front of me.

My eyes became transfixed on every glossy detail of a young adult woman, unclad in all her magnificence. It was a true trip to bountiful. (Although my sexual latency period would remain latent for several more years, the experience did in fact stir in me a profound desire to get on with the business of maturation.) As time stood still that night, however, I simply wondered, "What hath Randy wrought?"

After permitting me a fair amount of time with his father's hidden treasure, Randy asked, then pleaded, with me to let go of his father's magazine. "Come on, my dad's going to be home soon," he said. "You're bending it. I'll get in big trouble."

"Yeah, trouble." I murmured as I loosened my hand and eventually headed in the general direction of home.

The spell that Hugh Hefner had cast over me was still somewhat operative as I made my way into the confessional the following morning. As I knelt before our pastor, I suddenly turned my attention to Sister's admonition to link my sins with one of the Ten Commandments.

As I knelt in silence, the pastor interrupted, "Do you need me to help you begin your confession, son?"

"No Father, I think I can do this," I responded.

"Then please tell me your sins."

"Bless me Father for I have sinned. This is my very first confession. This is my sin."

Curious at my choice of words, he asked, "You have committed only one sin in your entire life?"

"Well I had a whole list of them, Father, but none of them seemed big enough to bother God about, especially after the big one I committed last night."

"What are you talking about?" he said. "What did you do last night?

For the love of God, tell me your sin right now." I sensed he was losing patience.

"Okay, Father. But can I start over?"

He waved his hand in exasperation, which I could see even through the screen between us.

"Bless me Father, for I have really sinned and this is my very first confession. This is my sin. I...."

My mind was racing over the Ten Commandments as if they were the final answers in a giant multiple-choice exam. I felt that if I did not plug my transgression into the correct slot I would never be forgiven.

"Father, last night, at my neighbor's house, I did something that I am very sorry for."

"Come now, child, tell me which of God's Commandments you have broken. What did you do at your neighbor's house?"

My mind continued to race over the Commandments as I began the process of elimination: first commandment, no; second commandment, no; three, four, five? My pulse quickened. This event was taking on biblical proportions.

"Father, last night at my neighbor's house I," my heart may have been in the right place, but my mouth refused to cooperate, "I, I...."

"Tell me what you did at your neighbor's house last night right now!" the priest insisted, raising his voice just enough that I was sure it could be heard outside the confessional.

"Father," I whispered, finally settling on the commandment that I had broken the night before, "last night I committed adultery!"

The Slowest Ship in the Convoy

Catholic children in Indiana learned the importance of currying favor with nuns at a very young age. The unwritten covenant between parents and teacher gave these women unfettered discretion. And through the eyes of us children, they were nothing less than courageous, willing to stand between their academic offspring and the razor sharp grip of Satan.

It was common knowledge, however, that the "good nuns" had gotten stuck on the lowest rung of the ecclesiastical pecking order. Indeed, they were not even allowed to distribute the report cards they themselves had authored. This was reserved for the highest-ranking church official in our mist. We knew him simply as "the Monsignor."

The report card ritual was remarkably predictable. As the Monsignor began his trek from the rear door of the rectory, a student strategically placed on the lookout would signal to Sister the priest's imminent arrival. His black cassock, lined with red, swayed in stark contrast to the freshly cut white stones of the cathedral he had built, brick by brick, with the donations of his immigrant parishioners. He slowly swaggered across the empty playground, where the ghosts of prepubescent energy still lingered from recess.

Sister anxiously observed his progress. With her patented "stare" she reminded each of us that if there were the slightest hint of insubordination in front of the Monsignor, we would be used as human corks to plug the portal to hell. (Of course, Sister would never actually say "hell.")

Then the moment would arrive when the Monsignor would disappear from sight. Presumably he was now in the school building. The second hand on the clock above the crucifix ticked slowly and loudly, waiting to be joined by the faint sound of his footsteps. As the doorknob began to move, and even before the door would completely open, we popped to our feet.

"Good afternoon, Monsignor!" we'd chant in perfect unison.

Our premature salutation was acknowledged with a token nod from the priest. Tall and gaunt, he was once heavier and taller. His solemn gray hair was combed back in a stately manner exposing a clear sign of intelligence. Sister stood off to the side, waiting for her vacant seat to be occupied. The class collectively sighed as his buttocks safely landed in the chair.

After a makeshift prayer, he was handed thirty-five freshly inked report cards. Mine rested on top because of our seating arrangements. (Mine being first seat, first row.)

His facial expression, as he perused each report card, always suggested how each student had done. Since I would usually do relatively well, the wrinkles on his forehead would signal levels of moderate satisfaction, rather than the deeper levels of consternation.

On this particular day, his more than modestly above-average positive expression suggested I had done better than usual, and I had. Not as well as Martina Gale, however. As she approached the Monsignor and they looked upon each other in mutual admiration, I took myself to an ongoing imaginary Indiana State High School Basketball Championship game featuring my athletic prowess as the main attraction for the thousands of onlookers invited to play extras in the production of my daydream. I had choreographed various endings that had me sinking winning baskets from every imaginable angle. By the time I had exhausted most scenarios that morning, only one report card remained to be handed out.

❧

The class braced itself for the inevitable disappointment the Monsignor would surely show after reviewing the grades of one Thomas Pillar. (Last seat, last row.) He was slight of build, with a genetic code that had not yet unlocked even a modest growth spurt. His brown eyes never seemed to be curious, making him appear humble for the wrong reason.

> *The Monsignor regularly reminded Thomas that "a convoy can only move as fast as its slowest ship."*

Usually, Thomas faced the Monsignor's verbal jabs quite well, because by the time they were filtered through his as yet undetected learning disability, he was already safely back in his seat. The Monsignor regularly reminded Thomas that "a convoy can only move as fast as its slowest ship." The Monsignor simply could not understand that this child had difficulty negotiating his way around a simple word problem, let alone a complex analogy.

On this occasion, however, Thomas Pillar would not be allowed safe passage back to the corner of the room. The Monsignor kept him in front of the class, badgering him with an unrelenting verbal assault. As Thomas began to process what was being said to him, his small frame began to shake. Oversized clothes, handed down from a brother missing in Vietnam, disguised his more violent trembling. He looked like a puppy who was not sure why he was being scolded, despite the wet spot in the carpet.

When Thomas began to weep, Sister Francesca breached ecclesiastical etiquette by intervening. She led the broken boy back to his desk, leaving behind not only the report card but also the man who, long ago, had forgotten why he had become a priest.

Building a Picket Fence
in a Pontiac

With all due respect, many Hoosiers are able to put basketball in perspective. Thank goodness our family was not among them. Indeed, my brother was blessed with the "b" gene, landing him smack dab in the center court of Hoosier hysteria.

What an eye Mark had for the greatest game ever nailed to the side of a barn or strung up above a garage door. He was the purest of shooters: confident, with a soft touch, easily able to go to the hole and score thirty plus points in back-to-back regulation thirty-two minute northern Indiana high school basketball games.

Much of my youth seems to have been invested in swaggering into high school gymnasiums of various sizes and smells to watch the best player to ever don a South Bend St. Joseph's High School basketball uniform. Greatly anticipated away games would take us to exotic places like Goshen, Elkhart, Kokomo, Fort Wayne, Gary and Michigan City.

Often the drives were in late autumn, when rural Indiana painted a hauntingly calm backdrop for the impending bitter winter. Storm windows on farmhouses were already locked into place, while trees and fields had already begun to settle into their state of hibernation. Late

October sunsets bled red as leaves in varying shades of the same color swirled like miniature tornadoes behind our black-and-white 1958 Pontiac.

My father drove in silence, wearing a soft smile and an expression suggesting he knew something the rest of us did not. The game itself was always a clinic. My brother would routinely silence the overly enthusiastic crowd of homers. And when the win was in the bag, the St. Joseph High School Band would come out of nowhere to taunt a disgruntled wad of hometown fans with several renditions of "When the Saints Go Marching In."

After having humbled the lion in its den, our family slipped back into the darkness and wound our way back to civilization. In the back seat of our car, sleep would overcome me—obviously the next in the Hurtubise line destined to carry our family's basketball torch to new heights. Even in my dreams, I was perfecting a shot even more perfect than the one that had come before it.

Everything else going on in the world was of little interest to me as I was growing up in Indiana. There was no need for me to build a great wall or tear one down. The picket fence I built in the back seat of that 1958 Pontiac was far more effective in keeping the outside world exactly where it belonged.

Packing Papa

The front porch swing that once moved in sync with balmy evening cricket concerts, hung motionless. There was the spot where the planted feet of my father had pushed me a million times. A deep chasm stood between that swing and the cab of the rental truck, where I waited to be transported to a new, but not better, house.

With arms locked I sat, still not yet having forgiven my father for having died in the dead of night, whisked away by paramedics—his arteries too hard to let the blood flow through them.

My older brother Mark put the last box on the truck. For a last time, he disappeared into the house, making certain what was left behind was less than garage-sale worthy.

Although the sun had not yet completely set on the horizon, it had begun to assume a reddish hue. My eyes turned to catch a final glimpse of green ivy tightly clinging to the red brick of our former home.

I could see inside the living room. Looking in from the outside, instead of looking out from the inside, was disconcerting. I could still see my father in his white vinyl chair, with a beer in hand and another by the leg of the chair. I remembered him trying to use animated gestures and mild curses to somehow influence the outcome of a pivotal University of Notre Dame football game.

This red brick fortress of my youth is always haunting, never haunted. It is where the infant Jesus was born over and over in a small makeshift stable nailed together by my father, and where the Easter Christ was in a perpetual state of resurrection on the living room wall.

As the rental truck started, it grunted and began its slow descent down Miami Street. Left behind were leaves waving in a familiar evening breeze, bidding farewell. A deeper reddish hue cast a warm glow upon bricks not yet covered by ivy.

The old house stood poised to begin molding new dreams for other children. My grip on it loosened as I began—even at that tender age—to understand that we choose to either live in the past or allow the past to live with us in the present.

Mark asked why I was smiling. I did not reply. I chose, instead, to give him a look suggesting I knew something he did not.

Sisters of Perpetual Nun-Chucks

The rental truck assumed full speed near the bottom of a hill on Miami Street, near Ewing, where houses were replaced by businesses. My brother Mark and I blew past Bush's Pharmacy, where the "aspirin in a Cherry Coke" scandal had been acted out. Eighth grade girls, painted with makeup, ushered in the sixties by crushing aspirin and mixing it into the popular soft drink. These young women would then pass out, falling from grace (as well as the fountain stools) while using their bodies like beakers in a chemistry class. When caught in this very act of testing a hypothesis, they were judged as being permissive in ways going way beyond a science experiment.

Down the road was the Stevens' Barber Shop. Mr. Stevens was a tall, handsome man, with a mustache similar to that of Clark Gable. On my way to school each morning, I knew to quicken, steady, or relax my pace depending on how far along he had shaved the same lather-faced man angled in his antique barber chair. Reserving for me a small space in the corner of his eye, Mr. Stevens, razor in hand, would offer me a warm smile.

This ritual was abruptly halted after an infamous Palm Sunday tornado, when Mr. Stevens' life was crushed while using his back, arms and shoulders as a makeshift fallout shelter to save the life of his son. From then on, even from the other side of Miami Street, the pall hanging over an antique barber chair obscured what remained of his warm smile.

～～

Our truck soon grunted past St. Matthew's Elementary, where we had all gone to school. Like Pavlov's dogma, our heads respectfully bowed in unison as we sped past the adjoining cathedral. This act of cranial genuflection spoke volumes of the depths to which the iron fists of the nuns kneaded our perception of God. Even to this day, at some level, I believe that the Almighty has more than a passing interest in seeing my spine and buttocks at a ninety-degree angle while sitting in a distant pew.

Sister Theresa felt using threats with children made less sense than blowing on an untoasted marshmallow.

Striking the fear of God into an undisciplined child was a tool teachers in the nearby public school did not have in their arsenal. The Sisters of St. Joseph were able to dispense divine wrath with the agility of a ninja wielding nun-chucks. Any ensuing semblance of order, however, was often purchased at the price of leaving children with incentive to give wide berth to any deity preoccupied with such a display of martial law.

～～

One day, however, a woman walked into the midst of my seventh grade class with grace and dignity. Her statuesque appearance and delicate features were the fodder an artist would need to capture the Madonna. Sister Theresa felt using threats with children made less sense than blowing on an untoasted marshmallow. She would find other ways to garner our attention.

A child, she felt, would have little interest in traversing the "wilderness within" if the ultimate recompense was being sucked into the spiritual vortex of some passive-aggressive deity. Instead, she taught us that the God resting within was not prone to anger. Through Sister Theresa, I discovered that those using threats of punishment and retribution were not describing God, but rather themselves.

When I told Mark what I had been thinking, he suggested it's best not to harbor any resentment toward the church. "Some day you'll probably figure out anger just gets in the way," he warned.

"Gets in the way of what?" I challenged.

"Saving your soul, I guess."

At first I was impressed by the simple yet irreconcilably wise insight of someone whom, I thought, had only been able to perfect a jump shot.

Then I remembered that when he had been in seventh grade he, too, had been taught by Sister Theresa.

A Peck in Time

When I was the age at which teenage boys agree only to disagree with adults on almost everything, one brave priest chose to step to the plate to teach us high school religion. Father Brennan sported a good solid middle-aged look—blond hair thinning and midsection thickening. Snug clothes suggested a metabolism slowing down more quickly than he was being issued new clothes at the rectory. His calm demeanor stood in sharp contrast to that of his students, the more bombastic of whom (myself included) had staked claim to all of life's answers.

Poised at the edge of his desk, he caught us off guard by voicing a disinterest in answers. His concern was discovering whether or not we were asking the right questions. To him, having answers without asking the right questions was like giving away ice in the wintertime.

As one would expect with adolescent boys, whose hormones were popping around like bingo balls in an air pocket, the most popular religion classes were those discussing sexuality and dating. Unwilling to acknowledge a connection between real relationships and dating a girl, most of us were more interested in knowing to what guilt-free windfall we were entitled once we found ourselves at "first base."

Father Brennan's unwillingness to reduce a budding romance to a sports analogy, however, should have warned us how meaningful a first date could be. Instead of arming us with a laundry list of "do's and

31

"don'ts," he invited us to contemplate the question, "Can conduct and consequences ever be divorced?"

Convinced his Socratic method was unresponsive to our more immediate need of knowing how to get to "first base" and, more importantly, what to do once we got there, our thirst for moral direction continued in the locker room. After some guidance from upper classmen, there was consensus formed that for "it" to qualify as an official "first base" point score, lips must touch more than casually. Also, the importance of the girl wanting to get to "first base" should not be underestimated. This had the added bonus of lessening the likelihood of any misunderstandings or hurt feelings.

After much discussion, we freshmen were let loose from the locker room into the wonderful world of dating. Our pact was to return and, without too much exaggeration, reveal our spoils.

≈

Felicia had jet-black hair so dark it exaggerated an already light complexion. Her green eyes were warm and curious. She was ahead of other girls on the maturation chart—in height and in other ways as well, making her look like someone's older sister. Dressing slightly provocatively afforded her much attention, at the expense of losing only a little respect.

After acting a bit surprised that I had asked her to be my first date, she quickly scribbled her address and phone number on the back of a matchbook cover. (That must mean she smoked too! I had hit the jackpot.)

Where Felicia lived, like so many homes in Indiana, made no pretense of being anything other than a fortress to withstand the bitter cold of winter. The solid brown oak front door was opened and closed quickly by younger versions of Felicia, twelve and four years younger, respectively. It seemed their charge was to keep me occupied while anticipation of Felicia was built into the complete dating experience.

The older of the two girls scolded the younger sister when she felt some social etiquette had been breached because I was given permission to hug the little girl's raggedy baby doll, limp from being loved intensely for one, maybe two, generations. The younger girl at first scowled and challenged her older sister's authority, but then she relented and hid behind a torn sofa in the corner so as not to be seen crying from embarrassment.

Felicia descended the stairs wearing a full-length, neatly pressed, plain flowered dress and well-polished black leather shoes.

From the older sister, I learned their mother was working a swing shift at a nearby factory. Their father had not been around long enough to leave a meaningful impression on them—or on the pictorial parade on the mantel over the fireplace, for that matter.

Felicia descended the stairs wearing a full-length, neatly pressed, plain flowered dress and well-polished black leather shoes. Her hair was set up in a bun, making it appear as though she may have expected to be taken somewhere more formal than anything within walking distance, which is where we were headed.

After a pleasant greeting, she flashed a look of maternal concern and asked, "Where's Penny." The older of the two sisters responded quickly, "Behind the sofa, being a baby again."

"Penny, you come here this instant." Felicia ordered in a way both gentle and firm that appeared to comfort both girls.

The small, obedient child slowly made her way from behind the sofa and found her way onto the lap of her oldest sister, gently holding her neck. One ear rested on Felicia's shoulder as her tear-stained eyes drifted across the room to see if I suspected she had been crying.

"Melody, I want Penny in bed by eight o'clock. Read to her and baby doll until they fall asleep, and then you can watch television. But nothing scary! Mom'll be home ten minutes after eleven sharp. So be in bed pretending to be asleep by then."

The evening itself was nondescript, yet in hindsight it should have been predictable. Felicia spent most of her time weaving and bobbing from my obvious advances, making every effort to engage me in conversation and learn more about my interests—hoping to discover in me a mutual interest in her.

I had no intentions, however, of deviating from my well-rehearsed and much-strategized game plan. Most of my energy would be spent plotting to bring back to the locker room the exaggerated spoils of my first date.

Sensing that the only thing I wanted to take away from our evening together was one casual kiss, Felicia consented early on. A little later, though, she said she had to go home and check in on her little sisters.

Before fading into her house and out of my life, and sensing in me the emptiness a boy feels when he wins a battle but loses the war, she took the initiative to kiss me a second time. It was just a token peck on the cheek, but of the two kisses I received that evening, as Father Brennan would have pointed out, only one would remain meaningful over time.

Basketball at the Rock

The last leaf of autumn clung tightly to a naked forest when I was summoned to the office of my high school basketball coach. This meeting was not unexpected, since Coach was asking to meet individually with his more promising players before he made a final cut.

As I strolled down the hallway to his office anticipating the admiration of those destined to concede my right of way, I attempted to temper the cockiness in my stride—something I knew I could only hope to contain. Coach, sitting behind the same metal desk every high school coach sits behind, asked me to close the door as he fidgeted with a paper clip. His demeanor was not one of wanting to massage the ego of a promising young athlete. I was told my skills would not mesh with those of the team. Wading through an outpouring of a well-intended clichés, I found myself on the other side of the snapped-shut door.

<hr/>

More than anything else, a teenager abhors embarrassment. Having lost my father and now, shortly thereafter, any purpose in my life, I was devastated. I knew that I had been sentenced to serve the remainder of my high school career as little more than a crease on the sleeve of anonymity. As providence would have it, however, someone would be

35

summoned to help me discover more about myself by helping me discover who I was not.

John Killeen was fresh out of the University of Notre Dame and in the infancy of his public high school teaching career when he moved next door to my now fatherless family. His straight blond hair always seemed about a week shy of a haircut. Tall and lean, he walked with his head slightly forward, making it appear that his direction always had purpose. From our living room window, he could often be seen dumping his gym bag in the back seat of his 1965 blue Mustang.

"Grab your gym stuff," he commanded. "We're going to the Rock to play some basketball."

Upon hearing I had been cut from my basketball team, John made a detour to our front door one evening before jumping into his car and speeding off to parts unknown. "Grab your gym stuff," he commanded. "We're going to the Rock to play some basketball."

"The Rock?" I asked.

"Yeah. The Knute Rockne Memorial Gym out at Notre Dame. It's been there forever. There's always a pick-up game. Mostly kids from back east. Most played in high school. Great hardwood floors. Lots of competition."

"I, uh, better do some chemistry homework." I hesitated. "I'm getting behind."

"I'll make a deal with you," John offered. "If you come with me, I'll help you with your chemistry when we get back."

"Well, maybe this once," I conceded as I ran to grab my gym bag that was still standing ready for what would have been the next high school basketball practice.

As we got into his car, something occurred to me: "How are you going to help me in chemistry? I thought you taught history."

"Yeah," he laughed, "But at Notre Dame they make you at least minor in intelligence. We'll figure it out."

It only took me that one time to get hooked on playing basketball at Notre Dame in a building named after a football legend. Most nights John and I would pile into his 1965 blue Mustang and head off to the Rock, followed by some chemistry cramming and topped off with a game of chess.

The Rock may have been the carrot, but the payoff was finding someone willing to rig a safety net for a free-falling juvenile.

My Spiritual Apprenticeship

Loyola University of Chicago is poised bravely beside the tumultuous waves of Lake Michigan. Giant slabs of concrete are the only barriers between academic freedom and the untamed forces of nature. Swells of storm water often mock this feeble mixture of cement, gravel and sand. White capped waves pound against the tightly sealed east windows of Cudahy Library, where attentive students are cautiously optimistic.

Also nestled against the jewel of the Great Lakes is *Madonna Della Strata* chapel. Built upon bedrock, the spewing of an angry sea is no match for what rests in its sanctuary.

Set back, away from the mischief of the lake, is the Jesuit residence. On it's front porch, in the evening air, a tired old Chicago Jesuit often shared thoughts with a kid from Indiana who had still not found a mission worthy of his life. Our meetings were only on warm evenings, when we could comfortably sit in large cast iron chairs designed to accommodate larger frames—and spirits—than mine.

One twilight, the wind over the lake calmed to a whisper. The old Jesuit was pensive. From squinting eyes propped up by several decades of laugh lines, he peered out to where the horizon and water met. His hands, leathery but without calluses, grasped the raw iron of the chair in a way suggesting his life was edging closer to winter.

When his massive body squirmed into a relative position of comfort, he began. "You need to know more about the spiral of anger," he told me.

"Whose, Father?" I asked.

"Yours, mostly. Be aware of all its faces. Of all our addictions, anger is the worst."

"Are you comparing anger to drugs or alcohol?"

"Yes."

"Why do you say anger is the worst?"

He was just warming up to the subject, one with which he obviously had first-hand experience. "Alcohol and drugs destroy the body," he explained, "but anger destroys the soul. What all addictions have in common, however, is the drive to keep themselves alive. Anger does so by gravitating to or creating violence."

"What kind of violence?" I asked. "Where people get physically hurt?"

"Physical assault is one aspect of violence. Violating an oath is also violent. Talking about people can be a violent act. Violence has many faces."

"Why are you telling me this, Father?"

"Forewarned is forearmed."

After a long silence, I tried to redirect his attention. "Tell me about the spiral of peace," I said.

"Although we're supposed to be made in God's image, we have a penchant for choosing the path of least resistance," he mused. "The other path, the narrow one leading to peace, tends to scare us. It requires commitment and sacrifice."

"What kind of commitment, Father?"

"Remember, like knows like. To stay in the spiral of peace, we must be sincere about being sons and daughters of God, and act accordingly."

"That's a big challenge, isn't it, Father?"

"You bet. Especially these days. The journey of becoming enraptured by peace competes with a culture packaging our humanity with the veneer of a television commercial. In a world of immediate gratification, there are those whose advantage it is to tell us *what* we are, instead of helping us discover *who* we are."

I helped him lift his tired old body out of the cast iron chair. We walked to the shore. There he stood in wonderment at something distant where the dark horizon met the water's edge.

And I? I continued my spiritual apprenticeship.

St. Frankie of Assisi

As the sun lifted its resonance from the frigid bed of Lake Michigan, Frankie would maneuver his way out of an exclusive lakefront residence, wind his way around the turn in Sheridan Road, and end up at Loyola University. There his "special needs" were allowed to blend into the seam of campus life. Thinning blond hairs were combed and locked in place with an odorless gel, often frozen like mini-icicles hanging like Christmas stockings from the hub of his wool cap. Thick glasses, often fogged, were poised on the bridge of a nose that ran especially hard in February. His chubby face, imperious to season, did not seem to need a wind chill to factor into the equation of his ruddy complexion. A gold and maroon book bag, displaying a Loyola Rambler, was packed with notepads, ruler and pencils. The fact that they were color coordinated with a light purple lunch pail suggested Frankie had a loving, if somewhat compulsive, caretaker.

A relationship with Frankie meant being open to a volcanic heart always ready to erupt. A simple nod of the head, shot in his direction, was the only incentive necessary to open the floodgates. As he scurried toward the person offering the gesture, his glasses would bounce on the bridge of his nose. The ritual was always the same: With feet planted, body steadied, head cocked and eyes locked and targeted, Frankie would sing, "Hiiiiiiiiiii! How are Youuuuuu?"

Then Frankie would wait in hopeful anticipation of permission to share—once again—the only moment in Chicago sports history having relevance to him. The script, with many variations, was something like this; "Frankie, do you have time to talk about the big game?"

The question would lock into place the common shred linking Frankie with those around him.

He would become animated. "Yeah, yeah! You know, you know! It was the big game!"

"When was that game again Frankie?"

"You know, you know, 3-23-63. The 3 means March. That's March 23, 63, 1963. You can remember cause 2 times 3 is 6 and you add a 3 at the tail of 63. It's like March, then 2 times 3 for the 6 in 63. Margot says if you let the 3 jump over the number in front of it like a frog you don't forget when Loyola Ramblers won over Cincinnati Bearcats."

"It was a great game, wasn't it?"

"Yeah, yeah!" he said, almost loosing his balance. "Loyola Ramblers beat Cincinnati Bearcats in overtime after regulation game of championship college basketball game. Iron Man Jerry Harkness made long ball basket to tie at end of real game."

"Jerry Harkness was All American, wasn't he?"

"Yeah! Yeah! Loyola Rambler Coach Ireland made him captain of Loyola Rambler team cause he's All American. Margot says after the big game a country was named after Loyola Rambler coach, but she laughed so I think she is making joke on me."

"Weren't the Ramblers down by fifteen at one point?'

"Yeah! Yeah! You know. They fought back. They never give up. Margot says never give up too like Loyola Ramblers didn't. Loyola Ramblers were losing fifteen points at Freedom Hall in Louisville, Kentucky, and came back to have same points as Cincinnati Bearcats. That is when Duke Blue Devil band came on Loyola Rambler side to help them win."

"Loyola beat Duke in the semifinals game, didn't they?"

"Yeah! Margot says Duke Blue Devils band was good sports cause Loyola Ramblers beat them earlier in semifinal game and then they gave their band to Loyola Ramblers to play music to help them win."

"What was that score of the Duke game, Frankie?"

"Don't know. No threes, but Les Hunter had almost thirty points in game against Duke Blue Devils. But Duke Blue Devils got over being beat real fast cause they wanted Loyola Ramblers to win over Cincinnati Bearcats bad. All the people were screaming loud for Loyola Ramblers."

"What happened in the overtime?"

"Little Johnny Egan jumps up way up in sky and beats big Cincinnati Bearcat basketball player for jump ball. Les Hunter misses big shot. I get real scared. But no worry, Vic Rouse will always be under basket to tip basketball into basket with no more seconds on the big scoreboard. It will always be 60 points for Loyola Ramblers and 58 points for Cincinnati Bearcats. Margot says score can't change anymore times."

～～〰～

Occasionally, I would take Frankie on a detour, away from the much-heralded moment at Freedom Hall in Louisville. Once, for example, I felt the need to tell him of Franco Zeffirelli's movie, *Brother Sun, Sister Moon*. The movie, depicting the life of St. Francis, mesmerized me into thinking my modest wealth—a pouch of ten silver dollars—should be somehow thrown back into the world.

I explained to Frankie how my plan of offering my largess to a man rummaging through trash was foiled when he began cursing at me as I approached him. "I tried to give him my silver dollars, but I guess he felt threatened," I said.

Wanting to help, Frankie began, "Margot says not everybody wants to hear about Loyola Ramblers championship basketball game against

Cincinnati Bearcats."

"I'm sorry Frankie, I don't get what your saying. What does the big game have to do with giving away silver dollars?"

Cocking his head, "You did not get permission from homeless man to talk about silver dollar coins. Maybe man did not want to talk about silver dollar coins. Margot says people's ears only let in stuff they want to hear. Margot would say silver dollars coin talk is only for people who love silver dollar coin talk."

Oddly enough, I realized that Frankie was right. "You know Frankie, I think you and this Margot person may have come up with something," I told him.

Feeling proud, Frankie continued, "Yeah, Yeah! Silver dollars coin talk is not for everyone."

"What I mean is that there is an old guy at the pawn shop I see all the time on my way to Loyola," I explained. "You know, at the Bryn Mawr station, under the 'el' tracks with a big 'COINS WANTED' sign up in his window."

"Yeah! Yeah! He looks like sad and mad man. I don't think he wants to talk about Loyola Ramblers basketball game, but maybe silver dollars coins."

"You stay here Frankie. I'll be right back. Thanks for you help."

As I walked away, Frankie advised, "Margot says be sure old man wants to talk about silver dollar coins."

My gait quickened as my blind Christian ambition gained momentum and new vision. The door to the pawnshop triggered the sound of a bell heard even over the noises of rattling trains shaking unclaimed merchandize once used to repay back rent and loan sharks. From the wrinkled face of an old man, like the watches, rings and money clips buried in a boxlike glass case he zealously guarded, hung many untold stories. As his head and hands were angled toward the case, the back part of his bald head displayed an atlas of liver spots. Only his eyes, hiding behind two small slits, moved instinctively as the bell clanged again when I shut the door.

I opened the pouch and laid my bounty of silver dollars side-by-side, careful not to scratch the glass counter.

Without any formal greeting, he spat in an unfamiliar accent, "What you got?"

My first attempt at explaining my Franciscan mission was drowned out by a roaring train passing.

As the sound of the train became a faint whisper, I opened the pouch and laid my bounty of silver dollars side-by-side, careful not to scratch the glass counter.

"You pawning or selling?" he asked with rehearsed disinterest, his eyes attracted to a single coin at the end, minted the century before.

"Neither. I'm giving," I explained.

His eyes, shaken from the single coin, looked up to study a beaming face he did not recognize in his mental filings of past negotiations.

"No, I'm serious. You got a sign that says 'COINS WANTED,' and I want to give you these coins."

Looking at me askance, he said. "Sign says 'COINS' not 'CONS,' Buster. What is your game? You with the police? My store is clean. Everything is registered."

"Whoa," I laughed, "I'm not with the police, I just wanted to do something nice for someone."

"Just in case you are with the police, take money and then we have a final deal," he said as his eyes gravitated back to the coin on the end.

"But I just want you to have them," I pleaded. "Do I look old enough to be a policeman? I'm barely out of high school."

"No money, no deal. That's final!" He snapped.

I relented, "Okay, give me whatever you want."

Ready to deal, he fell back into his element. "Coins not worth much, all scratched and worn."

"Well give me fifty cents apiece," I demanded.

"No good. It's token. Sounds like I'm still getting set up for something."

"Fine," I retorted sarcastically. "Pay me what you think is legal. Just make yourself happy, darn it!"

He cautiously began the art of bidding against himself. In the end, he agreed to pay no less than three dollars a coin, whereupon he threw down three soiled ten dollar bills and quickly snapped up the coin at the end and carefully buried it in his pocket. The others he threw in the box-like glass case.

"Now you leave my store and don't come back, ever," he ordered. "Take your receipt. I got copy too. So don't come back. We have deal."

I lumbered back to Loyola where Frankie was waiting where I left him. I gave him a nod.

"Hiiiiii! How are Youuuu?" he started.

I interrupted, "I'm fine, Frankie, but I'll tell you that shaking up the world is not as easy as it was for Saint Francis." His head, which initially was cocked at a forty-five degree angle to the right, evolved to a forty-five degree angle to the left as I explained to him what had happened.

After a long silence, Frankie concluded, "Maybe you should not watch Saint Francis movie again if it makes you be so carried away."

"You're probably right," I sighed. "But you know, Frankie, what I think I really need to hear right now?"

"No," he replied, hoping he might be able to help.

"I wish somebody could tell me about the big game."

An ear-to-ear grin appeared.

"I can! I can! Yeah! Yeah! You know! You know! It was the big game...."

Dr. Liss to the Rescue

Armed with quivers of curiosity, Loyola University of Chicago students freely moved into the windy city intending to perfect the art of challenging and being challenged. My own first off-campus epiphany was waiting for me a short distance up Sheridan Road and three short blocks down Devon Avenue just past Magnolia, where an eccentric old man was cultivating ideas like a good farmer cultivating fruit.

Dr. Liss had a remarkably straight spine for someone having celebrated his eightieth birthday over a decade earlier. His face was virtually wrinkle-free, save the multiple laughs lines jutting out of his clear blue eyes. His Baby Beluga-size heart was carried around in a body with less body fat than a retiring ballet dancer, and natural oils made thick white hair stay in place like the crest of a frozen wave.

Our first meeting was incongruous. He stood outside his business, a health food store, arguing with a full-bearded old rabbi who ministered at a nearby synagogue. I gravitated toward the elders, thinking I might be needed to placate what appeared to be an escalating situation. (Some men are known for choosing their moments of heroism recklessly. I usually choose situations where I am the youngest and the strongest person involved.)

They were spewing Hebrew, causing Yahweh, no doubt, to cover his ears. Arsenals of long bent fingers were slashing the summer air in each direction as if each were competing for the coveted position of conductor of the Chicago Symphony Orchestra.

More impressive than neither being hurt, however, was the long embrace they gave each other before the rabbi moved on.

Turning to me as if I had always been his confidant, Dr. Liss confided, "If being stubborn made such a man a karate master, he would have ten black belts to hold up his over-starched *tallis*."

"Yeah, but if you're so angry with him, why did you hug him?" I asked, skipping any formal introduction.

"You can't stay mad at a mule if it chooses not to make the journey," he sighed, begging the question.

"But what were you guys fighting about?" I persisted. "Was he trying to convert you to his religion or did it have something to do with the conflict in the Middle East?"

"No conversion; only conflict," he replied.

Changing directions, my new-found but as yet unnamed friend asked, "Where do you stand on fresh-squeezed apple juice?"

Bewildered, I asked, "Excuse me?"

"Come and have some apple juice and I will tell you about the rabbi," Dr. Liss offered, opening the door both to his health food store and to another world for an impressionable college freshman from Indiana.

Before consuming what to me looked like the garden variety apple juice my mother bought at the A&P, I was encouraged by Dr. Liss to close my eyes and see the rays of sunshine captured in each apple, dangling and swaying in a quiet orchard, courting gentle breezes blown from distant places where the sky was so blue in hue that impressionistic art would have been changed forever had Monet discovered a color so pure. Since the Chicago Jesuits were incessantly trying to teach me the importance of being respectful, especially to the elderly, I played along in his attempts at elevating the stature of an innocuous piece of fruit. Such was my introduction to someone whose greatest, and perhaps only, satisfaction was in healing others of their illnesses. I would learn that Dr. Liss was one of the great pioneers of the fledgling Chicago health food industry.

At the core of his beliefs was the notion that within each of us rages a great war—not only for our body but also our soul. Dr. Liss campaigned tirelessly, extolling the virtues of what I would later learn to be anti-oxidants and painstakingly fought to quell the tide of free radicals—decades before the *New England Journal of Medicine* did so.

"The lifeless food of man, for all its ill-gotten gains, will destroy human cells faster than we can build hospital cells," he told me.

It took very little time for me to appreciate that passion for life was the engine driving this eccentric man. Like other visionaries, Dr. Liss was an easy target when his zeal was written off as little more than a sideshow. "Peace will only come when world leaders discover their consternation comes from constipation!" he'd say, and my hip friends would groan.

Those willing to separate the whole grain from the hyperbole, however, were rewarded handsomely with better health and a healthier outlook. "I don't want a hundred grand a year, I want a hundred grand people a year!" he'd proclaim.

❧

Predictably, Liss Organic Foods was without pretense. The décor was early American general store. Large crates of cereals were priced not by the pound but by what the consumer could afford. "To become healthy, consumers must be allowed to consume!" he'd say. "Let the rich pay more so the poor may eat!"

A strong odor, more unfamiliar than unpleasant, met customers as they entered the store. The pungent smell, no doubt, came from the large jars of exotic teas, not completely hermetically sealed. Makeshift signs were strewn throughout the store. "WE RESERVE THE RIGHT TO MAKE YOU HEALTHY," "THE COLD IS THE CURE!" and "EAT BRAN! A REVOLUTION BEGINS WITH A MOVEMENT!"

Dr. Liss spent a sizable chunk of his time directing traffic from a rocking chair strategically planted in the most visible corner of his store. From this throne, he would skin peanuts, play his violin, recite poetry, or borrow freely from anyone he considered a friend—and there were many of us.

Visiting Dr. Liss became as much a daily ritual to me during my college years as putting on my socks.

Thrown in jail at least once for "practicing medicine without a license," Dr. Liss never did quite perfect the art of courtroom diplomacy: "I do not practice medicine, your Honor, I practice health. I implore you to find one ounce of medicine in my store. Leave the vials of medicine to the ones who brought me here today! The AMA is known to me from this day forward, your Honor, as the American Murderers Association!"

Visiting Dr. Liss became as much a daily ritual to me during my college years as putting on my socks. Lentil soup, steamed kale, sweet mango, or fresh squeezed fruit juice was always waiting for me after my classes. The greeting would always be the same. "What did the Jesuits teach you today?" he would ask.

"To be respectful to authority," I would suggest, mostly just to get a reaction.

"Just what the world needs, another robot," he'd say. "Go and eat your supper before the water bugs get it!"

Battling city officials became as expected a habit for him as rubbing his five o'clock shadow. I was not alarmed, then, one hot summer day, to see him engaged in lively debate with a Chicago police officer outside his store as a crowd assembled. He claimed he had waited all summer for the temperature to reach 98 degrees so he could conduct an experiment on the public sidewalk.

The temperature, he explained to the police officer, was the same as that of the human body. He promised to prove that a piece of steak he earlier had cooked in the oven would become rancid in less time than it otherwise would take for the human body to digest it. "If we can prove to the world the dead carcass of an animal begins to putrefy while still in the human digestive tract, it will be very significant indeed!" he told the officer, who appeared to have very little patience for the entire conversation. He wiped his brow and offered a sigh of relief when he spotted the long-awaited city health inspector.

While the two argued over who had jurisdiction over Dr. Liss this time (each conceding venue to the other), I asked permission to go in and help myself to apple juice. "By all means," the doctor said, "but don't forget to refresh your spirit as well!" Then he turned to meet the health inspector, an obese man whose cotton shirt had absorbed its full capacity of body sweat.

"Why if it's not Patrick Sullivan, Chicago's answer to health," he chided in a fake Irish brogue. "Elections are only five months off Patrick. Shouldn't we be out campaignin' on such a lovely summer day?"

"I have little patience for your antics today!" the inspector warned.

"Okay then, Patrick, but you will be lettin' me know when you're ready to become a healthy health inspector?" Dr. Liss continued to bait the man, returning to his regular voice. "Just look at you, half my age and twice the weight!"

"Don't start with me, Dr. Pine Nut," Sullivan retorted, in no mood to be reminded of his family's propensity for heart disease. "Now what in the holy name of Mother Mary are you up to this time? Only you could cause such a stir by dumping a fine cut of meat on the ground. Wasting perfectly good sirloin when so many people are hungry? What's gotten into you?"

"People hunger for health, not the ravages...."

I could faintly hear them continue to banter as I pulled down a large plastic glass, one perfectly suited to aid and abet in quenching a hearty thirst. Their words faded when I closed my eyes. For a long moment, I could see a quiet orchard where sun-drenched apples swayed in a light summer breeze. Only then did I begin to drink for the first time in my life.

Did Job Have a Job?

As the masses of Chicago huddled under blankets of goose down in buildings heated by old coal-stoked furnaces, I waited upon a platform in the middle of the night and prayed for a train to come and devour me into its warm embrace and take me home from work. This station was a sneeze away from the Illinois Masonic Medical Center, where I had just worked half a graveyard shift. As I waited for the "el" (as it is universally called in Chicago), my thoughts drifted away from my immediate chill and landed amongst the twists of fate that caused a Jesuit by-product to be working in a Masonic hospital.

A century before, freemasons would not have thought to hire and help a Catholic in his efforts to support himself through school. They were notoriously anti-Catholic and had secret signs as a means of recognition and exclusion. This history of secrecy smacked of intrigue, so when I was hired as a hospital "messenger" I was flattered to be entrusted with their "messages." Disappointment reigned, however, upon discovering the only messages I would carry were prescriptions to the pharmacy. Other of my job descriptions included hauling urine samples from nursing stations to testing labs and carting patients to their rooms after surgery.

Although humbled, my job at the hospital was one I had grabbed after having been discarded as political fodder by the Richard J. Daley political machine. My previous job had me hunting down death certificates in the Bureau of Vital Statistics. I was selected by a ward committeeman who was convinced I had "da right stuff" to be a part of "da finest political party in da history of mankind."

"Every time you gets in a car and puts it in gear," he told me, "da D stands for Democrat and that makes da car goes forward. Da R stands for Republican and makes da car goes backward."

Having "da right stuff" meant being able to harness the vote amongst the Loyola University student population who under the recently ratified twenty-sixth amendment to the United States Constitution were now permitted to vote at eighteen years of age. My job was perceived as a perfect plum of political spoil.

Such radical thinking was not only "a danger to Chicago but to the free world as well."

Youthful idealism, however, such as encouraging tolerance for opposite points of view, squared me off against this *crème de la crème* of all political machines, and idealism didn't stand a chance. The stuffing was knocked out of the committeeman's "right stuff" prophetic vision when I refused to leave my job during work hours and board a bus to the south side of the city to campaign for a candidate whose name and positions I didn't know. The ultimatum I was given, destined to stain my burgeoning curriculum vitae, was "either be bussed or be busted." A smile cracked my frozen cheeks when I suddenly realized how many times social consciousness had sprung from being told where to sit on a bus or when to get off a bus. Now my youthful conscience was being molded by being told so empathically to get *on* a bus.

The coffin of my political patronage career was nailed shut when I protested to the ward committeeman that using a tax-paid work force to further the political aspirations of a fledgling south-side Democrat might put his Republican opponent at a unfair disadvantage. His expression was timeless. Such radical thinking was not only "a danger to Chicago but to the free world as well."

~~~

Seeing my breath in the cold night air for some reason made me postulate that for all the grease in such a well-oiled political machine perhaps the trains really did not run on time. My thoughts fast-forwarded to a more recent event.

When I had arrived at a nursing station earlier that day to take my first assignment, I fully expected to be sent away with a vile of blood or bottle of urine. My limbs went numb, however, when a nurse instructed me to take a corpse in an adjoining room to a makeshift morgue in the basement.

"Excuse me?" I asked, hoping she had been talking to a nearby janitor who was mopping the floor.

"Take the woman to the morgue and put her in the cooler," the nurse ordered. "I've already done half your work by sticking her on the gurney. Her family won't leave until she's taken away. Now get going!"

"I don't think messengers are supposed to be wheeling dead people around," I argued.

She looked befuddled.

"I mean suppose she falls off the gurney. I don't think I'm qualified to be doing this sort of thing. I haven't had any medical training."

"If granny falls off the gurney, tell her to jump back on," she said, blending humor and sarcasm. "Now hop to it! The ER is bursting and we need that room."

I started toward the room. I heard weeping. I slowly opened the door to see a very large man in stained work clothes, tightly holding onto the dead woman's hand. A much younger woman was hypnotically brushing the dead woman's snow-white hair, which stood in stark contrast to her dark skin. Faintly, the young woman with the brush was singing a song. It was a song a grandmother might sing to lull a small child to sleep.

Unsure of the proper etiquette, I told the man holding on to the old woman that it was time to go. The young woman who had been brushing the woman's hair looked at me in a way that suggested I had a lot more answers than I had. As I left with the body, no one resisted.

My trek to the morgue was, predictably, uneventful. I even felt an eerie calm as I wheeled away the woman, who was still warm from the love of her family. As the elevator descended into the subbasement, for some reason I imagined how a stagehand must feel after the final curtain comes down on the career of a brilliant actress.

The rumbling of an ancient train covered with graffiti shook me from my freshly cut memory. It soon gave me a reprieve from the bitter cold. As I sailed past icy winds no longer able to touch me, I muttered a prayer for a family with whom I would, forever, be ever-so-slightly connected.

One, with Everything

S ilence stood in sharp contrast to more familiar Chicago street noises. The absence of sirens responding to midnight mischief, the hum of distant elevated trains, and nonsensical soliloquies offered by bold old men stumbling home in the dark from just-closed taverns was unsettling.

My college diploma was the first thing I unpacked from a suitcase testing the strength of a padded cot where the Trappist monks of Gethsemane, Kentucky, expected me to sleep while on a retreat to decide my future.

The week before, I had been advised to take the diploma, with ink dried like blood around a fresh cut, by a priest who encouraged me to keep the line moving after I became tentative about whether or not I was ready to proceed with my life without the Chicago Jesuits at my elbow. Drifting across the stage, I gazed upon the masses, small pockets of whom would scream when their family name was proclaimed over the loud speaker. Although my mother did not shout, I could feel her eyes fixed on me as I made the futile gesture of looking for her. After the ceremony I had no trouble finding this woman, whose glow was as easy for me to spot as the beams of light outside a theater on opening night.

After attempting to pronounce that part of the diploma written in Latin, my mother pulled from a bag my graduation present. The bag was not the kind received at a checkout counter but rather the more expensive kind, with gold stars hand-pasted against a blue paper sky.

The gift itself had been purchased when a mason jar, once used to seal stewed tomatoes, had become ripe with pocket change. It was a hand held tape recorder with earphones. Her act of utilitarian kindness had been purchased shortly after learning of my acceptance into the graduate program in journalism at Northwestern University.

≈

The monastic backdrop where I choose to reassess my decision to become a journalist was austere. The Trappists had made great strides in designing interior castles, but obviously knew very little of interior decorating.

The blueprint for my "cell," no doubt, had been borrowed from the Kentucky Department of Corrections. Had the door been ripped from its hinges and iron bars welded on, I would have felt haunting solidarity with murderers and car thieves indeed.

Although I knew monk logic did not factor creature comfort into their spiritual equation, I was not ready for these sobering surroundings. With lights out and locked in a fetal position on a cot fronting life's razor's edge, I continued the painful process of rediscovering who I was by rediscovering who I was not. As my eyes adjusted to the dark, the moon suddenly disappeared behind a lampshade-like cloud. My prayers were flung into the pitch dark, falling to the floor like darts thrown against an iron curtain. Conceding this dark night of the soul had nowhere else to go, I retreated quickly into the crevice between self-analysis and sleep.

Morning light brought yet another shade of austerity. Dressing quickly, I hurried to the cafeteria where world-renowned cheeses and breads had become as popular as the writings of former monastery resident Thomas Merton. I piled provisions on my plate, insurance against any stray packs of ravenous retreaters who might come to deplete the kitchen of its entire stock of coffee cakes and cheddar cheese.

This fear of imminent starvation proved unwarranted as the two men sitting at another table directly across from me were the only other ones to come to breakfast. Both were skinny, clean-shaven, bald-headed Asian men dressed in bright orange gowns. One was young and one was old. Each of their plates contained modest portions. When a monk came and offered them more, they graciously declined. As he passed, though, I reached out and added a third piece of warm cinnamon nut bread to my mound of comfort. The monk smiled at my act of aggression.

It wasn't long before an older monk, dressed in a well-pressed robe, came and swept the two guests through a door leading to the outside. As they left, neither chose to make contact with my curious eyes. Later, after having fully explored the surrounding thickly wooded area, I found myself trekking back to the monastery and sauntering down the well-trodden path leading to the grave of Thomas Merton. The site had become a true "tourist Trappist."

Alone, and with eyes locked upon a humble cast iron cross inscribed simply with "Father Louis," I had hoped the cross somehow had the clout to summon the great monk and author for some impromptu posthumous career counseling, but after admitting to myself that Merton had never been known for doling out career advice, I simply settled for the opportunity of being near him by sitting on top of his grave with my back squarely against the cast iron cross that was his tombstone.

~~~

After having allowed my spirit to surf the crest of many waves, the cycle was interrupted when I sensed I was no longer alone. My eyes could not open completely because the sun had moved in front of my face. It was not so bright, however, to keep me from recognizing the brightly colored orange gowns of the two men who had sat across from me at the table where I had eaten breakfast.

The translation resulted in a look of confusion over Kosei's face.

I jumped to my feet and apologized to them for, perhaps, not showing the proper respect for the grave site.

"It is we who should be apologetic for disturbing your meditation," offered the younger of the two men.

"Actually, I was just trying to relax," I explained. "I didn't sleep too well last night."

"Perhaps sleep will come better tonight," the monk predicted.

"Yeah, maybe."

As I brushed a leaf that clung to the lower part of my pants, I introduced myself. In kind, he responded, "My name is Rissho, and this is my teacher, Kosei."

The older man, who remained silent, bowed slightly rather than extend his hand. The younger of the two continued, "We are from Tibet and are on our way to attend a conference at the University of Chicago."

"Oh, I went to college in Chicago. Just graduated," I blurted out.

"Did you go to school at the University of Chicago?"

"No, I went to Loyola University."

As I spoke, Rissho translated my every word for Kosei.

"Kosei wants to know if you were doing the spiritual exercises of Ignatius Loyola when we came upon you."

"No, I never learned how to pray that way. But I did take a class at Loyola where a swami taught me how to do a breathing meditation."

The translation resulted in a look of confusion over Kosei's face.

"Let me try this again," I suggested. I paused to catch my breath. "The Chicago Jesuits at Loyola hired a teacher who was a swami and in his class we learned how to meditate."

After the translation Kosei sighed. That sigh needed no translation. "We have come here to the United States from Tibet to learn about your religion and share the information with the priests where we live," Rissho continued.

"Priests?" I interrupted with a look that suggested I, too, needed a translation.

"Oh, I am sorry. We are Buddhists," Rissho explained. "We live in a monastery, and it was there where Kosei convinced his teachers there is much to learn about the teachings of Jesus."

"Oh, I get it. The University of Chicago is having some kind of religious conference and they invited people from all over the world."

"Something like that," Rissho said warmly.

"But if the conference is in Chicago, why are you in Kentucky?" I asked.

As the question was translated, Rissho responded, "We have come to Kentucky to learn more about Thomas Merton. Kosei believes Thomas Merton was most enlightened."

"Yeah, he knew a lot of things about religion."

"Kosei adds, though, that Jesus was much wiser and more clever in many ways."

"Clever?" I asked, a bit defensively, never having heard Jesus referred to as being clever.

"Yes, Kosei says he tried to help his followers understand by teaching them to see from the vantage point of what he called heaven."

"Could you ask Kosei to explain more?"

After a brief discussion, Rissho continued, "Kosei asks if he can teach you like Jesus might teach you."

"Sure," I humored him. "Have him take a crack at it."

"Kosei wants to know from you whether it is easier to say 'your sins are forgiven' or 'take up your mat and walk'?"

Having that feeling of being hit with a pop quiz without having read the assignment, I tried to wing it. "Well, I think it was clear that Jesus would have thought forgiving sins was probably easier because sins can always be forgiven, but once you can't walk, well, then, I suppose that means that's it. I guess that means you can never walk again if you're paralyzed. But I'm not absolutely sure. I'm not sure there is an answer to that one. That may have been a trick question to get his disciples thinking."

I was clearly out of my league in this conversation.

My only hope was that my response would somehow become more profound after translation.

From the puzzled look on Kosei's face, it would seem Rissho had made an accurate translation. Before Kosei continued, he took off a part of his garment near the top of his robe. He spread it on the ground over where Father Merton rested. Getting down on his knees he made marks on opposite ends of the article of clothing.

"Kosei says to think one mark means 'Your sins are forgiven' and the other means 'Take up your mat and walk.'"

After Kosei sprang to his feet, he then had me asked, "How much distance is there between the two marks?"

"About, maybe three, four feet," I guessed.

"Kosei says you are correct as long as you see the garment while you are stuck to the earth."

Kosei bent down, picked up the garment, and held it vertically toward the sky. "Only when you see the garment from the vantage point of the one Jesus calls his Father in heaven does it become possible to see there is no distance at all between the two marks," Rissho explained. Kosei then slowly brought the two marks together.

"Kosei thinks Jesus was trying to say sin and paralysis are the same thing. Sin does not let you move back onto your path. You stay off the mark, disconnected from your true self."

"Oh," I said, suddenly realizing that I had nothing really to say. I was clearly out of my league in this conversation.

"Now Kosei wants to ask you another question," Rissho said.

"Oh, no," I thought, still processing the last, but timidly I said "Sure."

"Kosei wants to know what you recommend we do on our free time when we are in Chicago?"

I sighed, this time in relief. Even I could answer that question. "It depends. If you like art, the Art Institute is the best. It's huge though. Don't think you can see the whole thing in one day. Same with the Museum of Science and Industry. If you are interested in sports, you might want to go to a Cubs game. I could be wrong, but I think they are playing the Mets this week. The Cubs don't win much, but fans in Chicago don't seem to mind."

"We will learn why it is America's favorite pastime," Rissho added.

"And you can order dogs at the ball park," I suggested.

"Dogs?" Rissho asked quizzically.

"I'm sorry. Hot dogs. It's a traditional American food."

"Is that like, how you say, 'junk food'?"

"Boy, you got that one right," I admitted, realizing they were probably vegetarians.

Thinking of an old joke, I thought I would give it a go.

"I know you probably don't eat hot dogs, but if you do and the hot dog vender asks if you want one with everything, tell him you want the hot dog plain, because waiting to become 'one with everything' takes too long."

After a long translation, both men laughed loudly and, surprisingly, without much in the way of self-control. I couldn't believe that I had pulled off a pun in two languages.

"Kosei says instead of asking for a hot dog he will ask for tofu dog," Rissho promised, as he wiped his eyes of his tears.

Finally, the stately looking Trappist found my new friends and shuffled them off to their next destination. As they dropped from my sight, I once again positioned my back against the cross of Thomas Merton. This time, however, I began to pray as if I were praying looking down instead of looking up. Later that night, I would sleep peacefully and without interruption.

Humanity's Dipstick

In fairness, television never purported to be anything other than a vehicle through which enterprising executives peddle goods and services. The early networks were actually quite democratic in the way they decided to air programs. If more things could have been sold by packaging philosophy rather than Uncle Miltie, then great thinkers from Aristotle to Zoroaster would have been beamed into our living room and the greatest threat from parents would have been, "If you children don't finish your peas, I swear there will be no watching the reading from Thomas Aquinas' early memoirs tonight!"

Instead, as this new medium became our evolutionary dipstick, market share gravitated more toward Lucy and Gomer than Kant and Hegel.

But even while the goofy cast of castaways on *Gilligan's Island* became the first prototype of a survival show, I was intrigued with a percolating movement pricking the social consciousness of the seemingly oblivious American consumer. Its earliest roots in my consciousness could be traced back to when journalist Edward R. Murrow exposed to the nation the plight of the American migrant farm worker in the documentary *Harvest of Shame*.

By the time I returned from my monastery retreat and met with my student advisor at the Northwestern University School of Journalism, I had reviewed all the profound things I had learned or experienced to that point. For some reason, however, *Harvest of Shame* stood out above all else. Such was the power of television.

Dr. Yamashita, affectionately known to her students as "Mama Yama," had a round face and deep intellect. She listened actively to my uncertainties and concerns about journalism school and how, as a back-up plan, the Chicago Jesuits had already made arrangements for me to hook up with the fledgling farm labor movement in California.

After helping me make my decision, which couldn't have been all that hard since I had already made up my mind anyway, Mama Yama wished me well on my adventure to California to seek, if not my fortune, my destiny. She did find it humorous, though, that Edward R. Murrow, her fellow journalist, had played a role in helping me decide to go in a direction other than journalism. Conceding that life was full of irony, she pointed out that my scholarship, as well as my career in journalism, was being left behind for another student, poised precariously on the top end of a long waiting list.

Maybe that person was deciding to leave his or her job as an organizer to try journalism school.

Gates of Gold

The plane landed just as the sun was setting down into a peaceful ocean. As it slipped from sight, brilliantly adorned clouds, poised at earth's edge, bid farewell to their source of illumination. I was in San Francisco, where a young priest whose ministry was to tend to the collective spirit of migrant farm workers met me.

Based on a description given to me by a Chicago Jesuit, Father Garcia was taller than I had anticipated. A strong frame suggested he, in another uniform, could have been a middle linebacker. His deeply-set brown eyes did not appear to have toiled at anything unhappily. During our time together, his mission was to teach me Spanish. In the end, however, I must have been a disappointment to him, as I was only able to master such words as *"Coachella," "Delano," "Salinas,"* and *"San Joaquin"* and offer of few refrains of the *cursillo* song *"De Colores."*

His tolerance of me was exhibited in other ways as well. His eyes would not roll when he was asked for the name of whatever mountain range we happened to be passing. The response was always the same, offered with the same respectful intonation: "We here in California refer to those mountains as hills, amigo!"

On our first journey, Father Garcia was most curious about what Chicago Jesuits had taught on a variety of subjects. "What did the Jesuits say was the most important lesson we could learn from history?" he'd ask, taking his eyes off the road for a second too long.

"Well," I'd propose after a brief pause, "One did say that the odd thing about history is it's mostly about getting even."

"And by that he meant?"

"I think he was saying that we haven't quite figured out yet how to settle differences peacefully. The pattern seems to be our leaders are pretty much expected to react violently when pushed."

"Maybe that's how the expression 'when push comes to shove' got started," he suggested with a smile.

"Yeah, it seems easy for countries to get caught in the eye for an eye, tooth for a tooth cycle," I added.

"I know," he said. "I think it was Gandhi who said we'll all end up being blind and toothless if we keep that up."

I laughed nervously.

"What was the biggest concern of the Jesuits?"

"Well, one was pretty concerned about how we are moving at a much faster pace scientifically than we are spiritually."

"And that's bad?"

"He said that within a hundred years it will be as easy to make a nuclear weapon as it is now for a kid to build an erector set and that unless there is significant spiritual transformation we'll be in big trouble."

"I think I know what his concern was," Father Garcia interrupted. "It's kind of like waiting to see if we will survive long enough to enjoy the cure for cancer."

"Yeah," I agreed. "Or winning the lottery the day before the Second Coming."

Father Garcia then launched into my education on the farm labor movement in the United States: "In 1965, migrant farm workers began to organize a labor union that would give them the opportunity to bargain collectively with corporate farmers, although farm labor wasn't given the same protection under the National Labor Relations Act as other jobs. Farm workers suffer from low pay, dangerous pesticides, child labor, field accidents, no toilets or clean water. Stuff like that."

I noticed that the plethora of stoop laborers picking crops we were passing on our journey were beginning to blend into the landscape.

I noticed that the plethora of stoop laborers picking crops we were passing on our journey were beginning to blend into the landscape, losing their novelty through their ubiquitousness.

"How did you get interested in the problems of migrant farm workers?" Father Garcia asked.

"It's kind of hard to explain, but when I was just a child I saw a documentary about migrant farm workers, and I always wanted to try and help them in some way."

"Was it *Harvest of Shame?*"

I was surprised. "How'd you know? I asked.

"I remember that show too—Edward R. Murrow, wasn't it? From my experience, it was pretty accurate."

"I figured I wasn't going to get that darn show off my mind until I at least tried to help someone," I confessed. "Some of the Chicago Jesuits believed pretty strongly César Chavez and his union seem to the best solution for helping migrant farm workers."

"I know César," he said in a way that did not sound at all like name-dropping. "It is quite ironic. One side is trying to deify him and the other is trying to demonize him, depending on how they see themselves."

"How do you think history will see him?" I asked.

"He will always be seen as a humble man with an unquenchable thirst for justice. Probably one of the few in this century, maybe the next, who was willing to sacrifice his life for social justice."

"Do you think his union will survive?"

"Yes, as long as its thirst for justice survives the inevitable appetite for security."

Not much more was said about farm workers or César Chavez until we arrived at our first labor camp. Until then, I lost myself in the distance, where an eagle struggled against an unexpected current. With a slight tilt to his massive span, he began to soar effortlessly against a cloudless sky.

Learning the Language of Justice

A scrawny dog with knotted yellow fur limped on an infected hind leg toward our car as we came upon the first labor camp. An unconvincing bark at Father Garcia was the only act of aggression the mangy mutt could muster, and it was negotiated only as a token gesture to satisfy what was left in his quiver of territorial instincts. As the car door slammed shut, he became startled and retreated sideways, dragging his back leg.

On dirt, bleached by the sun, stood rows of steel shelters, some of which were precariously propped up on cement blocks. These metal mounds were reinforced with boards in places where steel had succumbed to the harsh elements. Besides the dog, dry bushes were the only other noticeable signs of life. The earth made an effort to cling to the shallow roots of the few that remained. In time, however, their fate too would be tied to the steady wind, breaking the bond and setting them free to tumble in a rootless world. Abandoned rust-stained cars would make a futile stab to block their passage.

As Father Garcia looked around, a look of concern overcame his face.

"Is there something wrong?" I asked.

"I don't know," he said. "Something doesn't feel right. Yesterday, I received a call about a little girl who had gotten real sick. She's supposed to be here." He scanned the deserted property.

"Come on," he suggested as he headed toward the far end of the camp. "Let's look over there."

Some of the housing units were without doors, let alone locks. We looked within each structure, but there was no one to be found. It was like a ghost town. "Isn't it strange?" I asked as we made our way through the camp. "Whoever put these houses up didn't put in windows."

"You use the word 'house' quite loosely," Father Garcia mused. "I don't think when they were built they had people in mind. It looks like some time ago there was a huge blue light special on giant tool sheds and someone just welded them together and called it a labor camp."

After an exhaustive search, Father Garcia suggested we get back into the car and look somewhere else. We left behind a trail of dust rising significantly higher than the ones left by drivers coming toward us. As I sat quietly, I became impressed at the size of the farms outside my window. They stretched on and on as far as the eye could see. Father Garcia pulled off the road and stopped on its shoulder. Alongside the fences of one of the corporate farms were many striking farm workers, waving red flags emblazoned with black Aztec eagles. The wings of the eagles were designed with ninety-degree angles.

Some of the strikers were shouting, *"Huelga!"* (I discovered later this means "Strike!") Others were engaged in a boisterous monologue with those who had crossed their picket line and were working in a nearby field. A Kern County Sheriff's vehicle was poised on the shoulder of the road, about a football field away, to remind all present of the long arm of the law.

Not knowing what to expect, I nervously attempted to engage Father in conversation, but he suggested I wait in the car as he tried to get more information about the sick child. As he approached the strikers, it was clear they knew Father Garcia and were excited to see him. After some dialogue, the priest moved from their midst and onto the field where others got up from their stooped position to greet him. Recognizing his Roman collar as a port in the storm, they too were happy to see him, but they did not give this onlooker the impression they knew him personally.

As he finished his conversation with the field workers, he could be seen giving them a blessing.

The workers in the field could be seen, from where I sat, leading Father Garcia to what looked like small metal barrels dumped alongside an open warehouse. Stillness overcame those previously screaming *"Huelga!"* as they watched the priest get more information about the little girl. As he finished his conversation with the field workers, he could be seen giving them a blessing. They, collectively, fell to their knees and made the sign of the cross. As the priest moved back toward the regiment of strikebreakers, he was again warmly greeted. An older strikebreaker accompanied him back to our car and politely opened the car door. As Father Garcia got into the car, the man whispered, *"Si se puede,"* which means, "It can be done." After spying me in the front seat, he acknowledged me with a warm smile and said, *"Vaya con Dios"*—"Go with God."

"Where to now, *Padre?"* I said, trying to come across a lot cooler than I was.

"I am afraid your tour is going to become a de-tour," he said. "We have to make tracks to Delano Community Hospital to check on a very sick little girl named Guadeloupe."

"Is she the one we're looking for at the labor camp?"

"Yeah," the priest responded, keeping both hands firmly on the wheel and applying more pressure to the gas pedal. "Guadeloupe is two or three. When she was playing near some empty barrels while her parents were working in the field she must have put her lips to one of the barrels that had been knocked over. They found her unconscious. When she wouldn't wake up, they rushed her to Delano Community Hospital."

"What had been in those barrels that was so toxic?"

"A pesticide, malathion."

~~~

When we arrived at the hospital, Father Garcia needed my assurance I felt comfortable going in with him. "I will warn you," he said, "once you open yourself up to this experience, you may not see the world the same way ever again."

Even in her coma, it was obvious this was a very pretty little girl. Her long jet black hair was thick; it encroached upon the brown skin near her high cheekbones. Her eyelids were locked in a half open position, showing only a pallid slit. Her thin frame was attached to a respirator that caused her frail chest cavity to move up and down in a wave-like motion. Father Garcia hugged the parents for a long time, and then he began to pray last rites over the child's body.

Perhaps because I felt I had no other recourse, I moved closer to Father Garcia and began praying with him, in a language I did not yet understand.

The Alert Citizen

Riding the planet with migrant farm workers lasted only one full revolution around the sun for me. At journey's end, the earth was still traveling around the sun at ten thousand miles an hour. From the experience, I had learned the world was not spinning out of control—only some of its occupants. As I departed, I was encouraged to remember, *"Cada dia es un regalo. Algunos dios son mas difíciles de abrir que otros."* ("Each day is a gift. Some days are just harder to open than others.")

A liberal arts degree and some quality time with migrant farm workers was the mighty thin glue holding my résumé together. Predictably, perspective employers were less than enthusiastic about my credentials. One employer in particular, scornful of my association with both the Chicago Jesuits and the migrant farmworkers, was quick to point out there was no room in his company for a "rogue's scholar." (Come to think of it, he had to be pretty sharp to come up with that pun.)

So as surely as birds fly back to Capistrano each March, my fledgling wings carried me back to Loyola University where, as so many times before, I sought the counsel of the Chicago Jesuits. Father Ed Sunshine, a theology professor, looked at my plight with his perceptive blue eyes. Earlier, this man had played a part in pioneering the Eighth Day Center for Justice, an organization intending to plant seeds of hope, but after a brief conversation it became apparent that he was going to be of little use in helping a confused young Loyola grad obtain a middle-management position, preferably with a six-figure starting salary. He did, however, alert me to an opening in a new federally funded program monitoring police activities.

≈

Citizens Alert turned out to be about as popular in police circles as a tofu burger at a meat packers' convention. Since the organization did, however, need someone to edit its newsletter, it would allow me an opportunity to impersonate a journalist. I

"We have finally found someone without a personal agenda."

applied for the position, even though it paid considerably less than six-figures. (Four was closer to the truth.)

The interview of me, conducted by the full board, was overlaid with suspicion. Distrust in me was born from their having discovered police informants monitoring their activities. *Agent provocateurs,* later disclosed as the Chicago police department's infamous "Red Squad," had infiltrated many churches and synagogues of social activists. What this sinister band of law enforcement officers were hoping to find never became clear to me. Perhaps it was to uncover the holy grail of blueprints outlining how a bunch of nuns, priests, ministers and rabbis planned to wrest power away from the Chicago Democratic Party.

Since I was a virtual unknown in the world of urban activism and probably had a minimally cop-like appearance (I was white, for one thing, and male for another, and Irish for a third), I did not take the suspicion of many board members personally. At most I found it to be curious and slightly paranoid.

Upon completion of my interview, however, a tall, attractive, middle-aged woman with dark skin and a bright smile stood and suggested that no more interviews were necessary. When asked why by others in the group, she responded, "We have finally found someone without a personal agenda."

≫

The woman's name was Ruth Wells. In the Deep South, where she was born and raised, Ms. Wells discovered that life, like jambalaya, can be just about as hot as you want to make it. She was always saying things I had to think about because I didn't understand them right away, like "Temper your spice, Jerry, because you're stuck with the stew long after the shrimp is gone!"

Never one to chase recognition, she warned her contemporaries, "Once the limelight gets into your eyes, it's easy to lose sight of where you've come from and where you're going."

Ms. Wells was more interested in results than fanfare. This was nowhere more evident than in the trenches of the "deep south" side of Chicago where she had gained notoriety by protecting the rights of homeowners by spearheading the Contracts Buyer's League. Ample poise and courage had made her the obvious choice to be appointed the executive director of Citizens Alert. Even Police Superintendent James Rochford, whose frustration with her at the police board meetings could be measured by the degree of ruddiness measured against his normally pale complexion, knew she was an indispensable element in reconciling the tumultuous police-community relationship.

A chunk of my time with Ms. Wells was spent investigating a "fleeing felon" statute, which gave police officers unbridled discretion to shoot a person fleeing after the commission of any crime the police judged to be a felony. This included young Percy Hawkins, who was shot dead by police while caught in the felonious act of stealing a bicycle.

Ms. Wells was painstakingly aware of the depth of sorrow felt by Martin Luther King, Jr., while he was dodging rocks, bottles and epithets when visiting Chicago. "Racial prejudice leading to hatred, no matter the color of the wrapping, is the same as cancer," she reasoned. "Its main goal is to destroy the very host giving it life."

Long summer days in the Marquette Park neighborhood were the rallying point for bigots throughout greater Chicago. There, they would assemble and strategize as to how they could most effectively "protect" local residents from unsuspecting motorists of color using "their" thoroughfares. What resulted were many motorists being beaten while attempting to traverse a newly carved municipal Mason-Dixon line drawn vertically at Western Avenue. The token police response suggested their tacit consent.

❦

One of my assignments was to cover an upcoming rally organized by the American Nazi Party and report on any alleged police indifference. American Nazis had discovered months before in the neighboring suburb of Skokie that by exchanging hooded sheets for swastikas, they could provoke more negative reaction and almost always be guaranteed a lead story on local and even national news. Amongst those rallying in Marquette Park, however, only a handful of the grown men present were willing to make the ultimate fascist fashion statement. Police presence was noticeably absent as I moved ghostlike among the crowd. Racist rhetoric was spewed from a makeshift grandstand atop the bed of a pick-up truck sporting a bumper sticker that read, "GUNS DON'T KILL PEOPLE, I DO!" What these unhappy bedfellows lacked in eloquence, they made up for in hate, often fighting with one another for a propriety stake in the megaphone. It wasn't long before, with one voice, they were no longer conspiring to communicate, but rather communicating to conspire.

The groundswell of hatred manifested itself in a plan to march lockstep to the outskirts of Marquette Park, where they would consummate their blood lust by beating as many black motorists as the law would permit. I snuck away from the crowd and ran toward Western Avenue to alert police. On my way, however, I found myself stopping to persuade minority drivers to turn around and steer away from the impending hornet's nest.

These repeated interruptions, however, allowed those marching behind me to catch up. My Paul Revere conduct was assessed as traitorous. Rocks rained down around me. Whatever athletic prowess I had retained from earlier days was put to the test as my fleet feet moved at record pace toward a flank of police officers. Rocks being hurled in my direction were soon being thrown at the police as well, which did in fact catch their attention. After having identified myself as a Citizens Alert representative and exaggerating a closer than real relationship with Superintendent Rochford, concern to protect both me and at-risk motorists was given immediate attention. Confident of a meaningful police response, I slipped away from the line of demarcation and back into the protective cover of urban obscurity.

〜〜〜〜

As I ran, however, I continued to duck out of the way of objects flying overhead until I realized that they were nothing more than sparrows. One object, however, was not a sparrow but a dirt clod coming close enough to me to explode at my feet.

Expecting to see an angry Nazi, I turned instead to see several black children standing ready to defend their turf from what they anticipated was an impending Nazi invasion. The leader of the kids shouted orders to his troops to stand behind the mountain of dirt clods stacked high upon a Red Flyer wagon. Paralyzed by the irony of the entire situation, I stood mute as dirt clods began to rain down around me. The closer they came to hitting me, the more arose cheers of delight from the youth.

The noise caught the attention of a frail, yet forceful, elderly black woman who screamed from the second floor of an apartment, "You children leave that boy alone! I saw he done nothin' to hurt you!" The barrage subsided and the children slowly dispersed. I will never really know for sure why. Maybe they respected the old woman. Maybe they had a change of heart because I was willing to stand my ground.

In any case, I learned that I was not going to help save the world as a bystander or observer. I would have to find another way.

How to Eat an Elephant

I guess it is predictable that my life's next great adventure was law school. What else was an idealistic young Catholic to do in those days? If I was going to change the world, it would be one case, one injustice, one law reform at a time.

So I got on a plane in Chicago and headed back to California and the University of San Francisco Law School. I felt completely alone, as the warmth of a friend's airport embrace had already faded. Tom Bacci, who always seemed to be there at every turn of my young life, intuitively knew my concern: "You have what's called approach-avoidance conflict, Jerry. The closer you get to something, the more you want to avoid going through with it. It happens a lot when guys are about to get married. It's seems a lot easier to be on one knee proposing than it is to be kneeling on two on your wedding day. But you know it's the right thing to do. You always have to get to that next level. Now get going!"

When I closed my eyes and relaxed my head against the soft part of the seat back, the plane's soothing vibrations were remarkably similar to ones I felt in my father's 1958 black and white Pontiac when I would fall deeply asleep in the back seat. Fear of flunking out of law school, however, wrested control of my sleep and lulled me into an altered state of consciousness.

"You look scared," a familiar voice whispered. In the seat beside me sat my cousin Kenny, oldest of the twelve cousins with whom I spent summers as a child on my grandfather's farm.

For some reason, I wasn't the least bit startled to see someone who had been killed years before in a car accident shortly after having gotten back from Viet Nam. "Well, Kenny, I know it's dumb," I said, "but after seeing movies like *Paper Chase* and hearing all the horror stories about the first year of law school, I don't know if I have what it takes. What if I flunk out?"

"What if the cow decides not to come back to us after he jumps over the moon tonight?" Kenny teased. "We won't have any milk tomorrow, now will we?"

His hand gently rested on my arm after I gave him a look of concern. "Look, Half Pint," he continued. "I'll tell you for the last time. If you want to succeed at life, you've got to stop beating yourself down with questions that begin with 'what if.' You got plenty on your plate dealing with 'what is' and right now you don't even know if the 'what is' is a good 'what is' or a bad 'what is.'"

〜

Airplane turbulence shook Kenny and I out of the dream. I rubbed the sleep from my eyes. The curtain of clouds below had been lifted and exposed a world of snow-capped Rocky Mountains. After taking a deep breath, I experienced a surge of confidence that overpowered any remaining traces of my traitorous fear.

As the plane surged westward, more confidence arrows began to fill my quiver. Not the least important of which was an arrow given to me by Sister Theresa in seventh grade.

"What was it you said, Sister, about problem solving?" I asked. I closed my eyes and saw her face—the face an artist would attempt to capture when painting the Madonna. "What was it we should ask ourselves as we stand before a challenge? What was it? Oh yeah: 'How do you eat an elephant?'"

"That's it, Jerry, you got it! And the answer will always be the same," she said as she fidgeted with her habit. "The only way to eat an elephant is one bite at a time. Just one small bite at a time."

Schooling with John Nolan

Brooms used for sweeping generalizations were collected and stored outside Kendrick Hall at the University of San Francisco before a fresh crop of eager young law students were allowed safe passage into the building. When all were safely inside, professors, some having had pitched in the Ivy League, began their craft of chiseling into our collective concrete consciousness the art of lawyering—a monumental task to be accomplished in only three short years.

As the doors behind us banged shut, the real world was left to reason in its own irrational way. We, on the other hand, would be left to reason according to dictates of law: no more simple thinking; simply legal reasoning—applying evidence to law, arguing a conclusion, and being aware, all the while, of the subtle nuances along the way affecting the outcome.

Being able to reason legally meant being willing to discard bias. Insulating ourselves in a new way of thinking was not only mandatory, it was a condition precedent for anyone wanting to become a lawyer. Those unwilling to submit would be sent home with the handle of their broom lodged squarely between the cheeks on their lower forty.

If God created saints for their purity, children for their innocence, and the poor for their humility, the creation of first-year law students was direct evidence of a divine sense of humor. To us, it no longer mattered how many angels could dance on the head of a pin. What was relevant to us was whether these alleged seraphs were trespassing and had assumed the risk of their sophomoric conduct. If they were injured, was it foreseeable? Or if these unruly cherubs had been there for a certain measure of time had rights vested in them to possess the surface of the pin or was it simply public property or maybe an easement? Or was this a crossover intellectual property matter, instead of a real property or tort issue?

> *For the most part, those in the legal and non-legal community alike give first-year law students wide berth the second time they attend the same cocktail party.*

The vast array of insecurities of first-year law students becomes most evident when they are seen attempting to convince anyone whose ear they can bend how convincing they can be. For the most part, those in the legal and non-legal community alike give first-year law students wide berth the second time they attend the same cocktail party.

"I don't mean to be disrespectful, Sir," I would say to someone whose eyes had already glazed over, "but you're not suggesting there is only one cause for the homeless problem? It might cut the mustard to talk about one cause for one effect in an undergraduate philosophy class, but in law school we learn to think differently. It becomes clear that for every social problem, there might be hundreds of causes. Let's get into the real world here, man! I need a lot more information to work with. Tell me about which homeless person your talking about, and then maybe, just maybe, we can talk about cause and effect for that one person. But even then, you have to talk about the many causes for that one person being homeless before you go talking about why he's on the street. See how these problems are more complicated than the untrained mind can imagine?"

~~~

John Nolan, an Irishman, husky and bright, was made to study law as Michael Jordan was born to play basketball. Legal reasoning flowed through his stream of consciousness with as much fluidity as the wind sings beneath the wings of an eagle drifting over the desert floor. Before a relevant legal principle could escape his razor-sharp grasp, it had been digested, stored, and made ready for recitation. From his athletic frame, with wavy red hair usually challenging the direction it was combed, he would listen to lectures as if he were channeling Clarence Darrow.

Perhaps it was my use of expressions like "Stop giving away ice in the winter" or telling stories about the "Hoosier who wouldn't go to a house of worship until they built a round church, because then the devil couldn't corner him" that caused John to gravitate in my direction.

Perhaps too it was because he had proven himself an accomplished baseball player and had heard rumors of my fictitious induction into the Northern Indiana Sports Hall of Fame.

No matter, we would become a study group of two.

"Do you think Professor Putz taught it the way I am explaining it?" he would ask.

"I don't know, John." I'd admit. "I think so. Explain it again. But this time don't go so fast. You know I can't write as fast as you can talk."

"Come on Jerry, this is the fourth time around."

"I know, I just want to make sure you get it right."

"Okay, One more time. In order to have subject matter jurisdiction...."

John's practical ways of explaining relevant legal principles still resonate through my legal consciousness: "Come on, you can get this stuff. It's easy. Think of it this way. You're from Indiana. When you were a little boy did you ever wake up in the morning after a first snow-fall?"

"Yeah, but what's that got to do with distinguishing direct from circumstantial evidence?"

"Just humor me. Now close your eyes. Let's pretend before you went to sleep you looked out the window and there wasn't any snow on the ground. But when you woke up, the ground was covered with snow. Even though you didn't see it snow, the fact that it's all over the ground is circumstantial evidence it did snow while you were sleeping."

"Okay. Go on."

"Now, pretend you woke up in the middle of the night, looked outside, and actually saw it snowing. That's direct evidence!"

"Oh." I murmured. My eyes, like so many times before, had been opened by John Nolan.

Only by happenstance did John ever suffer a grade as low as an 'A-' in his illustrious law school career. Fortuitously, it came to pass in our Constitutional Law class, where I received the only 'A' I would receive in law school. (I made it widely known that if I knew he was struggling so much in the class, I would have spent more time tutoring him.)

The secret to John's success was his appreciation of the principle "familiarity breeds confidence." He specialized in the efficient use of time to commit to memory thousands of relevant legal principles. This, we both learned, had more to do with motivation than intelligence.

"It's not the one percent inspiration that scares me," he joked. "It's the ninety-nine percent perspiration. Anyone sweating that much is going to end up stinking the place up!"

Commitment without motivation was doomed from the start, John believed. Otherwise, he suggested, just play the home version of failure. Stay in bed and have someone else walk the tuition money to the mailbox.

John Nolan's gift for those willing to be swept up into his energy was his unrelenting enthusiasm for every challenge he faced. Before each law school exam, he would smile at me and wave his clenched fist to make certain I knew I would not be alone in slaying the dragon.

Before I ever stepped one foot in the law school at the University of San Francisco, I already knew from my Irish ancestors that something worth having is worth the struggle to get it. It is John Nolan, however, who—even until this day—will not allow me to forget it.

John died at age forty-one over ten years ago in Fairfield, California. I mark the end of my spiritual apprenticeship on the day of his burial.

Going Up? Going Down?

Most freshly cut lawyers often attempt to convince juries of the futility of their way of seeing the world and the value of adopting a new vision. More seasoned attorneys will simply work with juries by writing them a new eyeglass prescription.

Sowing résumés in the land of subtle persuasion was like watching autumn leaves falling off an old maple tree. Once settling on the hardening earth, the fate of only a few would be ironed between sheets of wax paper and preserved with others, from seasons past, in a leaf collection.

"There is not much room left in your leaf album," my mother would warn as I neared adolescence. "This year, only pick one or two leaves that stand out."

The field of applicants vying for the coveted position of Deputy City Attorney in San Francisco was stacked high and deep—much like autumn leaves waiting to be incinerated. It was common knowledge in law school circles that landing such a job was choice, since it meant gaining instant trial experience while being mentored by some of the most learned professionals practicing law in northern California.

Armed with a modest *curriculum vitae* and donning a new "law" suit that had been snatched from the tailor without the benefit of discovering that the trousers had been hemmed way too high, I swaggered into an interview intent on "standing out" amongst a sea of applicants.

≈

It is not completely clear to me how I responded to the hiring committee's first question about what made me the most qualified applicant to represent the City and County of San Francisco, but I do remember their confused look when I had finished my answer. I think I worked into my response how back on the farm in Iowa Kenny said pay no mind to my doubts when distinguishing "what if" questions from the more important "what is" questions. I'm also sure I must

Each person on the hiring committee gave the others a blank look.

have added something about how I was open to constructive criticism because—as the Chicago Jesuits used to say—people, like institutions, whose ideas do not permit self-critical thinking almost always substitute arrogance for analysis.

Each person on the hiring committee gave the others a blank look.

After a moment of silence, the chairman spoke up: "Well, thank you for coming in, but as you know this position is subject to the approval of the Board of Supervisors and they don't decide for a few months."

I blurted out, "What if I volunteer until then?"

Startled, he explained, "I don't think you understand. The Board doesn't vote for months and there is no guarantee the position will even be approved."

"Look, what's it going to hurt?" I began respectfully. "Think of it as a residency. It will give you a chance to see if I'm a good fit if a position becomes available. If I'm not, I'll thank you for the experience and you can hire one of the other applicants."

Committee members looked at the chairman for guidance, but there was none forthcoming. No one had ever offered to work for free before. Finally, David Goldman, one of the younger and more respected attorneys in the office, broke the silence. "I've got a huge drug-bust-gone-bad case against the cops on next month's trial calendar and need a ton of research done," he said.

A more senior attorney shot a look at Mr. Goldman that suggested I should not be encouraged.

Before Mr. Goldman could be politely admonished, however, John Etchevers, who headed up a complex litigation team, chimed in, "Mayor Feinstein's slander suit has been appealed, and I could use some help too." Pausing to study my résumés, he added, "It looks here like the applicant knows something about constitutional law."

Sensing dissention among his ranks, the chairman suggested I wait in the hall so the matter could be discussed privately. I walked out slowly, hoping no one would notice the direction my dyslexic tailor had hemmed my new trousers. As I passed Mr. Goldman, he offered an encouraging smile.

The hallway had been turned into a makeshift waiting area, where my solid navy blue suit stood in stark contrast to the more complex sea of pin stripes neatly tailored and perfectly worn by the other young men waiting their turn. A look of curiosity overcame the audience of applicants as I, instead of leaving, sat down and crossed my legs, accentuating my knee-length wool socks, which were fortunately the same shade of blue as my suit.

Sounds from the other room were active, but muffled, like lively yet inaudible bantering between priest and penitent on the other side of a confessional. When the noise subsided, I recognized the profile of Mr. Goldman moving closer to the frosted glass part of the door. As I was invited to step back in, he, with his back turned to the others, gave me a wink.

Begrudgingly, the chairman announced, "Some here think they

could use your help. But by no means are you guaranteed a spot when—and if—a job becomes available. Your work product will be monitored very closely. We have over two hundred applications for this position."

"Thank you very much for the opportunity," I beamed, knowing full well a team of wild horses would not be able to remove the foot I had successfully gotten in the proverbial door.

"Another thing," the chairman ended, "for God's sake, find yourself a better tailor!"

I found my way through the marble corridors of City Hall to an elevator. As fate would have it, Mayor Dianne Feinstein herself was standing next to me, poised to share the same elevator. She couldn't help but notice the beaming young man wearing a new blue suit with short trousers. Both her bodyguards sized me up more as a curiosity than a threat. They, like the mayor, simply smiled.

Having already broken more than my share of workplace rules that day, I chose to remain quiet. I will admit, however, it was tempting to let her know I had just landed my first real job as an adult and that I was looking forward to being one of her new lawyers.

There would be plenty of time for that later.